THE THEATRE GUILD

presents

A Musical Play

Based on the play
"'GREEN GROW THE LILACS'" by Lynn Riggs

Music by

RICHARD RODGERS

Book and Lyrics by

OSCAR HAMMERSTEIN II

Production directed by ROUBEN MAMOULIAN

Production under the supervision of
Theresa Helburn and Lawrence Langner

Musical Director	*Costumes by*	*Settings by*
JAY S. BLACKTON	MILES WHITE	LEMUEL AYERS

Dances by AGNES DE MILLE

Orchestrations by RUSSELL BENNETT

VOCAL SCORE

(Edited by ALBERT SIRMAY)

Vocal Selections also available (HL00312292)

ISBN 0-88188-039-6

First performance at the St. James Theatre, New York
March 31st, 1943

OKLAHOMA!

Cast of Characters

AUNT ELLER......................................Betty Garde

CURLY..Alfred Drake

LAUREY...Joan Roberts

IKE SKIDMORE...................................Barry Kelley

FRED...Edwin Clay

SLIM...Herbert Rissman

WILL PARKER....................................Lee Dixon

JUD FRY..Howard da Silva

ADO ANNIE CARNES...............................Celeste Holm

ALI HAKIM......................................Joseph Buloff

GERTIE CUMMINGS................................Pamela Brittan

ELLEN..Katharine Sergava

KATE...Ellen Love

SYLVIE...Joan McCracken

ARMINA...Kate Friedlich

AGGIE..Bambi Linn

ANDREW CARNES..................................Ralph Riggs

CORD ELAM......................................Owen Martin

JESS...Vladimir Kostenko

CHALMERS.......................................Marc Platt

MIKE...Paul Shiers

JOE..Harold Gordon

SAM..Arthur Ulisse

TIME:
Just After the Turn of the Century.
PLACE:
Indian Territory (Now **Oklahoma**)

Synopsis of Scenes

ACT I

SCENE 1.   The Front of Laurey's Farm House.

SCENE 2.   The Smoke House.

SCENE 3.   A Grove on Laurey's Farm.

ACT II

SCENE 1.   The Skidmore Ranch.

SCENE 2.   Skidmore's Kitchen Porch.

SCENE 3.   The Back of Laurey's Farm House.

*Musical Program**

                                                                    Page

Overture   5

ACT I

1. Opening Act I (Oh, What A Beautiful Mornin') 16
2. Laurey's Entrance 23
3. The Surrey with the Fringe on the Top 24
4. Kansas City 37
5. Reprise of "The Surrey with the Fringe on the Top 50
6. I Cain't Say No 52
7. Encore—I Cain't Say No 57
8. Entrance of Ensemble 61
9. Many A New Day 63
10. Dance—Many A New Day 70
11. It's A Scandal! It's A Outrage! 77
12. People Will Say We're In Love 84
13. Change of Scene 91
14. Pore Jud Is Daid 93
15. Lonely Room 99
16. Change of Scene 104
17. Dream—Sequence

    (a) Melos 106
    (b) Out of My Dreams 108
    (c) Interlude to Ballet 113
    (d) Dream Ballet 119
18. Entr act 135

ACT II

19. Opening Act II—The Farmer and the Cowman 140
20. Farmer Dance 154
21. Change of Scene 159
22. All Er Nothin' 160
23. Change of Scene 175
24. Reprise of "People Will Say We're In Love" 176
25. Change of Scene 179
26. Change of Scene 181
27. Oklahoma 183
28. Encore—Oklahoma 198
29. Finale Ultimo 205
30. Outmarch 209

*(Condensed from orchestra score by Jay S. Blackton)

Overture

RICHARD RODGERS

Opening Act I.
(Oh, What A Beautiful Morning)

Words by
OSCAR HAMMERSTEIN II

Music by
RICHARD RODGERS

bright, gold-en haze on the mead - ow, ___ There's a bright, gold-en

C-523-

haze on the mead-ow, ___ The corn is as high as an el - e-phant's

(Curly enters)

eye, An' it looks like it's climb-in' clear up to the sky.

Stgs. *pp* a tempo + Cls. + W.W. *poco rit*

29 Moderato

Oh, what a beau-ti-ful morn - in' Oh, what a

Stgs. W.W. Guit. *p* a tempo

beau-ti-ful day ___ I got a beau-ti-ful feel -

in' Ev - 'ry - thin's go - in' my way.

All the cat - tle are stand - in' like stat - ues,_____ All the

cat - tle are stand - in' like stat - ues,_____ They

don't turn their heads as they see me ride by, But a
lit - tle brown mav - 'rick is wink - in' her eye.

Oh, what a beau - ti - ful morn - in',

Oh, what a beau - ti - ful day,

I got a beau-ti-ful feel - in',

Ev - 'ry thin's go - in' my way.

+ Hns.

W.W.
Stgs.
Hp.

L.H.

Hp.

81 CURLY: *"Hi-Aunt Eller"*
ELLER *"Scare me to death! What're you doin' around here?"*

CURLY: *"Come a-singin' to you"*

Cl.

Stgs.

All the

8va

p a tempo

sounds of the earth are like mu - sic, _____ All the

8va

Bls.

W.W.
Stgs.
Hp.
Hn.

Oh, what a beau - ti - ful day, ____

I got a beau - ti - ful feel - in',

Ev - 'ry - thin's go - in' my way, ____

rit al fine

Oh, what a beau - ti - ful day. ____

sempre rit

pp Hp.

Ped.

Laurey's Entrance

No 2

Cue: Curly: Yeow, you too!

C-523-

The Surrey With The Fringe On Top

Cue: Curly: If I was to ast you, they'd be a way
to take you, Miss Laurey Smarty.
Laurey: Oh, they would?

17 Tempo giusto

CURLY:

Chicks and ducks and geese bet-ter scur-ry When I take you

out in the sur-rey When I take you out in the sur-rey with the

fringe on top! Watch thet fringe and

see how it flut-ters When I drive them high-step-pin' strut-ters!

C-523-

Nos - ey - pokes -'ll peek thru their shut-ters and their eyes will

pop! The wheels are yel-ler, the up - hol-ster-y's brown, The

dash-board's gen-u - ine leath - er, With i -sin-glass cur-tains y' can

roll right down, in case there's a change in the weath - er.

Brightly

AUNT ELLER: (spoken)
Would y' say the fringe was made of silk? _____

CURLY: (sings)
Would-n't have no oth-er kind but silk _____

LAUREY:
Has it real-ly got a team of snow-white hors-es?

CURLY:
One's like snow, the oth-er's more like milk. _____

AUNT ELLER:
"So y' can tell 'em apart!"

poco rit

+ Hns. Guit.
mod⁰ marcato

C-523-

Birds and frogs-'ll sing all to-geth-er and the toads will hop! The wind-'ll whis-tle as we rat-tle a-long, The cows-'ll moo in the clov-er, The riv-er will rip-ple out a whis-pered song, and whis-per it o-ver and o-ver:

Stgs.
W.W.
Hns.

pp

85

L'istesso tempo

AUNT ELLER:
I'd shore feel like a queen settin' up in that carriage!

CURLY:
On'y she talked so mean to

me a while back, Aunt Eller, I've a good mind not to take her.

LAUREY:
Ain't said I was goin'.

CURLY:
Ain't ast you!

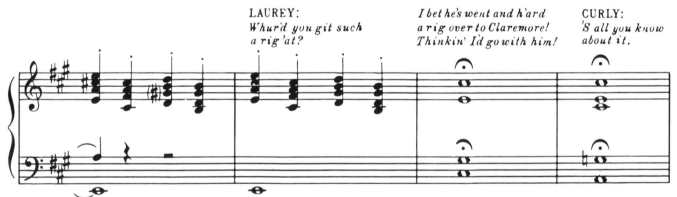

LAUREY:
Whur'd you git such a rig'at?

I bet he's went and h'ard a rig over to Claremore! Thinkin' I'd go with him!

CURLY:
'S all you know about it.

LAUREY:
Spent all his money h'arin' a rig and now ain't got nobody to ride in it!

CURLY:
Have, too! Did not h'ar it. Made the whole thing up outa

my head.
Vn.

LAUREY:
What! Made it up?

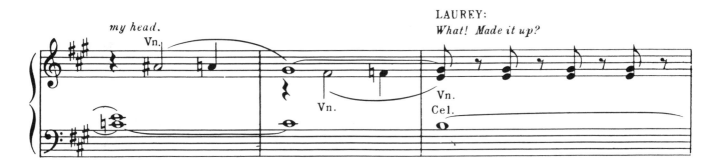

CURLY:
Dashboard and all.

LAUREY:
Oh! git offa the place, you!

Aunt Eller, make him git hisse'f

CURLY:
Makin' up a few-look out now! Makin' up a few purties
ain't agin' no law 'at I know of. Don't you wish they was
sich a rig, though?

outa here. Telling me lies!

'Nen y' could go to the play party and do a hoe-down till. mornin' if you was a mind to.
'Nen when you was all wore out, I'd lift you onto the surrey and jump up alongside of you.

And we'd jist point the horses home _ I can jist pitcher the whole thing.

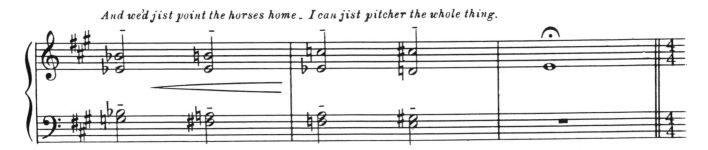

C-523-

Nod - din', droop - in' close to my shoul - der till it falls, ker -
plop! The sun is swim - min' on the rim of a hill, The
moon is tak - in' a head - er, And jist as I'm think - in' all the
earth is still, A lark - 'll wake up in the med - der.

C-523-

Cue: Will: But I shore did see some things I never see before.

sky - scrap - er sev - en stor - ies high _____ A -
ay - ter they call a bur - lee - que _____ Fer

bout as high as a build - in' or - a grow. BOYS: *(whistle)*
fif - ty cents you c'n see a dand - y show.

A boy: Girls?

53

Ev -'ry-thin's like a dream in Kan - sas
One of the gals was fat and pink and

Cit - y _____ It's bet - ter than a
pret - ty _____ As round a - bove as

WILL (*starts two-stepping*) IKE: *Whut you doin' Will?*

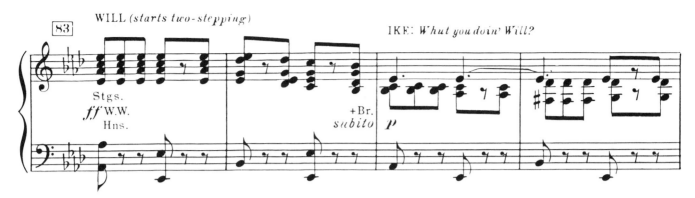

WILL: *This is the two-step. That's all they're dancin' nowadays. The waltz is through. Ketch on to it?*

A one-and-a-two, a-one-and-a-two. Course they don't do it alone.   *C'mon, Aunt Eller.*

(*Will dances Aunt Eller around.*)

Reprise of

The Surrey With The Fringe On Top

Cue: Aunt Eller: "Lands, you did?"

Moderato

CURLY: "Shore did. Purty one, too. When I come come callin' fer you right after supper, see

that you got yer beauty spots fastened onto you proper, so you won't
lose 'em off, you hear. At's a right smart turnout.

CURLY:
(sings)

The wheels are yel-ler, the up-hols-te'r-y's brown, The dash-board's gen-u-ine leath-er, With i-sin-glass cur-tains y' c'n roll right down, In

C-523-

case there's a change in the weath - er.

17 CURLY: *(speaking)*
See you before to-night

Stgs.

pp

anyways, on the way back from the station.(he starts to leave)

CURLY: *(sings)*

Ain't no fin - er

rig I'm a think - in' 'at I'd keer to swop for that

(Curly exits singing last note)

shin - y lit - tle sur - rey with the fringe on the top.

dim.

ppp

(no rit)

C-523-

I Cain't Say No!

Cue: Ado Annie "Yeow, they told me."

Trio

Whut you goin' to do when a fel-ler gits flirt-y and starts to talk purt-y, Whut you goin' to do?

S'pos-in' 'at he says 'at yer lips 're like cher-ries, er ros-es er ber-ries, Whut you goin' to do?

S'pos-in' 'at he says 'at yer sweet-er 'n cream and he's got-ta have cream or die?

Whut you goin' to do when he talks thet way? Spit in his eye?

Encore-I Cain't Say No!

No 8   # Entrance Of Ensemble

Cue: Ado Annie: You do talk purty!

(Will tries to kiss her)

No, I won't!

got-ta git a kiss an' it's got-ta be quick, Er I'll

jump in a crick an' die!

ANNIE:

Whut's a girl to say when you talk that-a-way?

16 ENSEMBLE ENTERS

Cue: Laurey: "What do I care about that?"

C-523-

on-ly man a-mong men. I'll snap my fin-gers to show I don't care, I'll

buy me a brand new dress to wear, I'll scrub my neck and I'll

brush my hair And start all o-ver a-gain.

Refrain

26 Con grazia - non legato

Man-y a new face will please my eye, Man-y a new love will find me,

Nev-er-'ve I once looked back to sigh o-ver the ro-mance be - hind me,

Man-y a new day will dawn be-fore I do! _____

Man-y a light lad may kiss and fly, A kiss gone by is by - gone,

Nev-er -'ve I asked an Au - gust sky,

C-523-

"Where has last Ju-ly gone?" Nev-er-'ve I wan-dered

through the rye, Won-der-in' where has some guy gone,

Man-y a new day will dawn be-fore I do!

LAUREY:

Nev-er-'ve I chased the hon-ey bee who care-less-ly ca-

joled me, Some-bod-y else just as sweet as he,

cheered me and con-soled me. Nev-er-'ve I wept in-

to my tea o-ver the deal some-one doled me,

Dance-Many A New Day

(Dance continues)

SINGING GIRLS:

Man-y a new face will please my eye, Man-y a new love will find me. Nev-er-'ve I once looked back to sigh

Tutti
mp

O - ver the ro - mance be - hind me, Man - y a new day will

dawn be - fore I do! _____

Nev - er - 've I chased the hon - ey - bee who care - less - ly ca -

W.W.
Hns.
Hp.
Perc. Stgs.

joled me. Some - bod - y else just as sweet as he

cheered me and con-soled me. Nev-er-'ve I wept in-to my tea

Tutti

O-ver the deal some-one doled me, Man-y a new day will dawn,

Bls.
W W

Man-y a red sun will set, Man-y a blue moon will shine be-fore I

Stgs.
W.W.
Hp.
Hns.

+ Bls.

Tutti
rall.

(All exit)

do. ————————

f a tempo

Cue: Ado Annie "Wait till I tell the girls."

(Ali Hakim, throws his stick,
and starts to pace up and down)

C-523-

I'm minding my own business like I oughter; Ain't meanin'any harm to anyone.

I'm talking to a certain farmer's daughter, Then I'm look-ing in the muz-zle of a

gun! It's get-tin' so you cain't have an-y fun,

Ev-'ry daugh-ter has a fa-ther wtih a gun.

Allegretto

Refrain 58

Men: It's a   scan - dal! _____   It's a   out - rage! _____   How a
Men: It's a   scan - dal! _____   It's a   out - rage! _____   Just a

Tutti *mf*

gal   gits a   hus - band to - day _____ *Ali Hakim:* If you   make   one mis-
wink   and a   kiss and you're   through _____ *Ali Hakim:* You're a   mess   and in

+ Br.

take   when the   moon   is   bright, Then they   tie you to a   con - tract, so you
less   than a   year,   by   heck! There's a   ba - by on your shoul - der, mak - ing

w.w.

110 *Girls, who have entered unseen during second refrain, lead men off, who follow unwillingly.*

People Will Say We're In Love

Cue: Laurey: No, Most of them say that you're stuck on me!

lect - ing things _____ *(Curly: Like whut?)* Give me my rose and my
night with me _____ Till the stars fade and from a -

glove. _____ Sweet - heart _____ they're sus -
bove. _____ They'll see _____ it's al -

Stgs.
W.W.
Hns.
Perc.
Hp.

pect - ing things _____ Peo - ple will say we're in
right with me _____ Peo - ple will say we're in

Tutti   *mf espr.*

1. *rit*

love. _____

2.

love. _____

f

segue after pause

End of scene

JUD appears
Stgs.
Eng.Hn.
Cls.

CURLY: (spoken) *Don't you reckon y' could tell that Jud you'd rather go with me tonight?*

LAUREY: *Curly! I—no, I couldn't.* CURLY: *Oh, you couldn't? Think I'll go down here to the
smoke-house, where Jud's at. See whats so elegant*

about him makes girls wanta go to parties 'th him.
LAUREY: *Curley!* CURLY: *What?*   LAUREY: *Nothin'.*

Laurey watches him off, then sits on rocker crying softly and starts to sing.

Laurey dries her eyes, picks up bottle of "Elixir of Egypt" and runs through the gate.

AUNT ELLER (Hums)

Curtain

attacca

Change of Scene

Moderato
(Play till next scene is ready — then fade out)

Piano

Pore Jud Is Daid.

Cue: Curly: They'd shore sing loud though when the singin' started, sing like their hearts ud break.

JUD:
And se-rene.

rene _____ He's all laid out to rest, with his hands a-crost his chest, His

fin-ger nails have nev-er been so clean!

17
CURLY:
(speaks)
'Nen the preacher'd git
up and he'd say:

(Chanting on one note)

(speaks)

"Folks! we are gethered here to moan
and groan over our brother Jud Fry who

hung his-se'f up by a
rope in the smoke house."

'Nen, there'd be weepin' and
wailin' from some of those womern.

(sings on one note)

'Nen he'd say, "Jud was the most
misunderstood man in the territory.

People use ter think he was a mean ugly feller. And they
called him a dirty skunk and a ornery pig stealer."

But the

(Chanting)

folks 'at real-ly knowed him, *knowed 'at beneath them two dirty shirts he always* wore, there

beat a heart as big as all out-doors. **JUD:** As big as all out-

CURLY: doors. Jud Fry loved his fel-low man. **JUD:** He loved his fel-low man.

CURLY: *(speaks)*

30 *He loved the birds of the forest and the beasts of the field. He loved the mice and the vermin in the barn, and he treated the rats like equals, which was right.*

And he loved little children. He loved ev'body and ev'thin' in the world! On'y he never let on, so nobody ever knowed it!

38

CURLY:

Pore Jud is daid. Pore Jud Fry is daid! His friends-'ll weep and wail for miles a-

W.W.
Stgs.
Hp.
Hns.

JUD:

Miles a-round.

CURLY:

round. The dais-ies in the dell, Will give

out a diff-'rent smell, Be-cuz por Jud is un-der-neath the ground.

C-523-

98

No 15

Cue: Jud: What am I doin' in this smokehouse?
a-crawlin' and a-festerin'?

The floor creaks, The door squeaks, There's a field-mouse a-nib-blin' on a broom And I set by my-self, like a cob-web on a shelf, By my-self in a lone-ly room. But when there's a moon in my win-der And it

slants down a beam 'crost my bed, Then the

shad-der of a tree starts a-danc-in' on the wall And a

+ Hns.

dream starts a-danc-in' in my head. And

all the things that I wish fer Turn

out like I want them to be   And I'm

bet-ter 'n that smart Al - eck cow - hand   Who

thinks he is bet - ter 'n mė!   And the

27 girl that I want ain't a-fraid of my arms, And her

C-523-

all a pack o' lies! I'm a-wake in a lone-ly room I

44 Allegro

ain't gon-na dream 'bout her arms no more! I ain't gon-na leave her a-

lone! Go - in' out-side, Git my-self a bride,

Git me a wom-ern to call my own.

Change of Scene

Moderato

(Play till next scene is ready — then fade out)

Piano

Dream Sequence
a) Melos

Moderato

Girls laugh.

VIVIAN:
And to yer house a dark clubman!

Piano

LAUREY: *(enters)*
Girls, could you, could you go some'eres and tell fortunes? I gotta be here by myself.

GERTIE:
Look, she bought 'at ol' smellin' salts the peddler tried to sell us!

LAUREY:
It ain't smellin' salts. It's goin' to make up my mind fer me. Lookit me take a good

whiff now! (She coughs)

GERTIE:
That's the camphor.

LAUREY:
Please girls, go away.

ELLEN:
Hey Laurey, is it true you're lettin'

Jud take you tonight stid of Curly?

LAUREY:
Tell you

better when I think ever' thin' out clear, Beginnin' to see things clear already.

KATIE:
I c'n tell you whut you want.

C-523-

b) Out Of My Dreams

Tempo di Valse

VOICE

Piano

I GIRL:
Out of your dreams and in-to his arms you long

to fly_____ II GIRL: You don't need E - gyp - tian

smell - in' salts to tell you why!_____

+ Br. W.W.
Vibra.

Cls.
Stgs.
Hp.

17 I GIRL:
Out of your dreams and in-to the hush of fall -

Cls.
Stgs.
Hp.
Vibra.

45 *(all girls in unison)*

Make up your mind, make up your mind, Laur - ey, Laur - ey dear._____ Make up your own, make up your own sto - ry, Laur - ey dear. _____ Ol' Pha - roah's daugh-ter __ wont tell

W.W. Stgs. *mf*   + Hns.   + Br.   W.W. Stgs.   + Hns.

61

you what to do, _____

Ask your heart _____ What - ev - er it

tells you will be true. _____

W.W.
Hns.
Trb.

poco rit

79 LAUREY: (as girls exit)

Out of my dreams and in - to your arms, I long to

Stgs.
Hp.
p a tempo

+ W.W.

fly_____ I will come as eve-ning comes to woo a

wait-ing sky._____ Out of my dreams and in-to the

hush of fall-ing shad-ows___ When the mist is

Curly enters L. and stands still, looking across

at Laurey.

low_____ and stars are break-ing through___ Then out of my

The counterparts of Curly and Laurey

enter and stand behind their originals, duplicating their gestures.

dreams I'll go _____ In - to a dream _____

Tutti

W.W.
Stgs.
Hns.
Hp.

with you. _____

+ Br.

Ped.   *Ped.*   *Ped.*   segue

c) Interlude To Ballet

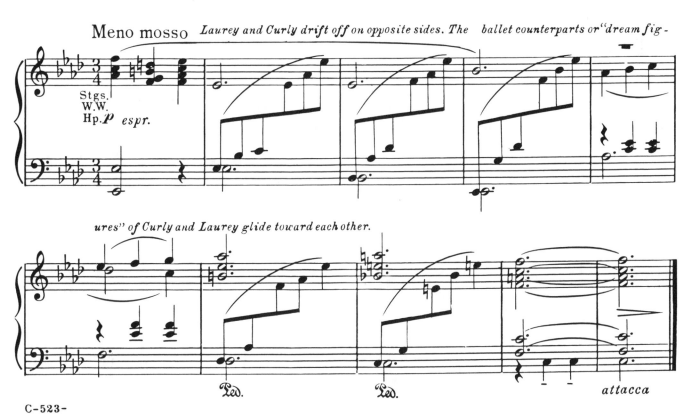

Meno mosso   *Laurey and Curly drift off on opposite sides. The   ballet counterparts or "dream fig-*

Stgs.
W.W.
Hp. *p espr.*

ures" of Curly and Laurey glide toward each other.

Ped.   *Ped.*   *attacca*

d) Dream Ballet

Tempo di Valse moderato *(The dream figures of Laurey and Curly dance ecstatically)*

Allegretto

"Laurey" and "Curly" keep on dancing

Grandioso

"Curly" kisses "Laurey" and walks away. Vns.

*A little girl presents "Laurey"
with a nosegay.*

Ben moderato

143 *More girl friends dance on and embrace her.*

A bridal veil floats down from the skies and they place
it on "Laurey's" head.

Andantino religioso *"Curly" awaits his bride who walks down an aisle formed by the girls.*

251

"The Wedding"

W.W. *p*
Chime

+ Hp.

(Vns.)

Sostenuto ed espressivo *"Jud" walks slowly forward and takes off "Laurey's" veil.*

Moderato

Subito molto allargando

poco   a   poco   accell.

a tempo

C-523-

Allegro *(one step)*

(cross hands)

481 Agitato *(in 2)*

W.W.
Stgs.
Hp. *f*
Timp.

(Hns.
Br.)

(Hns.
Br.)

Tutti

Exit

Grandioso (*in 4*)

"Jud" chokes "Curly" to death and carries "Laurey" off

The real Jud awakens Laurey from her dream and starts to go mechanically with him. The real Curly enters expect-

antly, and seeing them leave, he stands alone, puzzled, dejected and defeated, as the curtain falls.

C-523-

End Act I

No 18

Con grazia

Orchestra

Piano

Subito piú mosso

63 Moderato

Tutti
mf

attacca
Opening Act II

Opening, Act II.
The Farmer and the Cowman

No 19

21 Curtain (*All dance*)

Tutti

37

f

121

farm-er and the cow-man should be friends,_____ Oh, the

farm-er and the cow-man should be friends._____ The

cow-man ropes a cow with ease, The farm-er steals her but-ter and cheese, But

that's no rea-son why they cain't be friends!

Cl.
Stgs.
Perc.

+ Hn.

𝆑 Tutti

sto - ny; _____ He rides for days on end with jist a po - ny for a

ADO-ANNIE:

friend __ I shore am feel - in' sor - ry for the po - ny. _____

Tutti

167

AUNT ELLER:

The farm-er should be so cia-ble with the cow - boy, _____

f dim. p Stgs. Cls. + Br.

_ If he rides by and asks for food and wa - ter, _____ Don't

CARNES:

treat him like a louse, Make him wel-come in yer house, But be shore that you lock

up yer wife and daugh-ter!

Repeat under dialogue until fight starts.

Tutti

mp

185

(Start here when fight begins)

ALL: *(who are not fighting)*

Oh, the farm-er and the cow-man should be

mf Tutti

f

friends, _____ The farm-er and the cow-man should be

C-523-

IKE:

that's no rea- son why they cain't be friends, _____ And

212

when this ter- ri -to-ry is a state, _____ And

Stgs.
Cls. *p*
+ Br.

jines the un -ion jist like all the oth -ers, _____ The

farm- er and the cow-man and the mer -chant, _____ Must

AUNT ELLER:

all be-have their sel's and act like broth-ers._____ I'd

228 Meno mosso

like to teach you all a lit-tle say-in',_____ And learn the words by

heart the way you should,_____ I don't say I'm no bet-ter than

a tempo

an-y-bod-y else, But I'll be damned if I ain't jist as good!_____

Farmer Dance

Change of Scene

Cue: Aunt Eller: "Pick that banjo to pieces"

No 22

All Er Nothin'

Cue: Will: You gotta stop havin' fun!
         I mean with other fellers.

ca - pers   When I was off in Kan - sas Cit - y

Mo._____   I heard some things you could-n't print in

pa - pers _____   From fel - lers who been talk - in' like they

know!   Foot!   I on - ly did the kind of things I

go and sow my last wild oat! I cut out all she - nan - i - gans! I

save my mon-ey, don't gam-ble or drink, in the back room down at Flan-ni-gans! I

give up lot-sa oth-er things a gen-tle-man nev-er men-tions, But be-

fore I give up an - y more, I wan-ta know your in - ten-tions!

do! _____ I'm a one wo-man man, Home lov-in' type,

All com-plete with slip-pers and pipe. Take me like I am er leave me

be! _____ If you cain't give me all, give me

Tutti

nuth-in' _____ And nuth-in's what you'll git from

ANNIE: me! Not e - ven sum - p'n? WILL: Nuth - in's whut you'll git from

me!

(*Will starts to walk away, nonchalantly, Ada Annie follows him*)

Tutti

I cain't be "in be-tween?" It cain't be "now and then?" No half and half ro-mance will do!

Would you build me a house, All paint-ed white, cute and clean and pur-ty and bright? Big e-nough fer two but not fer three!

WILL: Uh-hu!

ANNIE:

Sup - pos - in' 'at we should have a third one? _____

WILL:

He bet - ter look a lot like

ANNIE: WILL:

me! The spit an' im - age! He bet-ter look a lot like

(Two girls enter and dance with Will)

me. _____

181

(*Annie stamps her feet*) Hey!

men like you are wild and free. _____ So I

219

ain't gon-na fuss, ain't gon-na frown, Have your fun, go out on the town,

Stay up late and don't come home, till three, _____ And

go right off to sleep if you're sleep-y _____ There's

WILL:

no use wait-in' up fer me! Oh, Ad - o An - nie!

235

ANNIE

WILL:

No use wait-in' up fer me! Come on and kiss me.

f

dim.

poco   a   poco   pp   attacca

Change of Scene

Reprise "People Will Say We're In Love"

No 24

Star - light _____ looks well on us _____

Tutti

Let the stars beam from a - bove _____

Who cares _____ if they tell on us? _____

LAUREY:
CURLY:

Let peo - ple say we're in love. _____

f espressivo e poco allarg.

sff

attacca

Change of Scene

Moderato
(Play till next scene is ready – then fadeout)

Piano

No 26   # Change of Scene

Cue: Ado Annie: Hello Will.

Moderato

(Play till next scene is ready - then fade out)

Piano

Oklahoma

Cue: Curly: Scared he wouldn't say it!

Gon-na give you bar-ley Car-rots and per-tat-ers Pas-ture for the

cat-tle Spin-ach and ter-may-ters! Flow-ers on the prair-ie where the

June bugs zoom — Plen-'y of air and plen-'y of room —

Plen-'y of room to swing a rope! Plen-'y of heart and plen-'y of hope!

land we be-long to is grand! _____ And when we say:_____

Tutti

ALL:
Yeow! A-yip-i-o-ee-ay! _____

CURLY:
We're on-ly say-in', "You're do-in' fine, Ok-la-ho-

ma! Ok-la-ho-ma! _____ O. K."_____

105 2nd Special Chorus

Encore - Oklahoma

wheat can sure smell sweet, When the wind comes right be-hind the

wheat can sure smell sweet, When the wind comes right be-hind the

wheat can sure smell sweet, When the wind comes right be-hind the

+ Cls.

21

rain. _____ Oh _____

rain. _____ O _____ k - la - ho-ma, Ev-'ry

rain. _____ O _____ k - la - ho-ma, Ev-'ry

Tutti *f*   *p* Stgs.
Perc.

Ev-'ry night we sit a - lone and

night my hon-ey lamb and I, Ev-'ry night we sit a - lone and

night my hon-ey lamb and I, Ev-'ry night we sit a - lone and

talk and watch a hawk mak-in' la - zy cir-cles in the

talk and watch a hawk mak-in' la - zy cir-cles in the

talk and watch a hawk mak-in' la - zy cir-cles in the

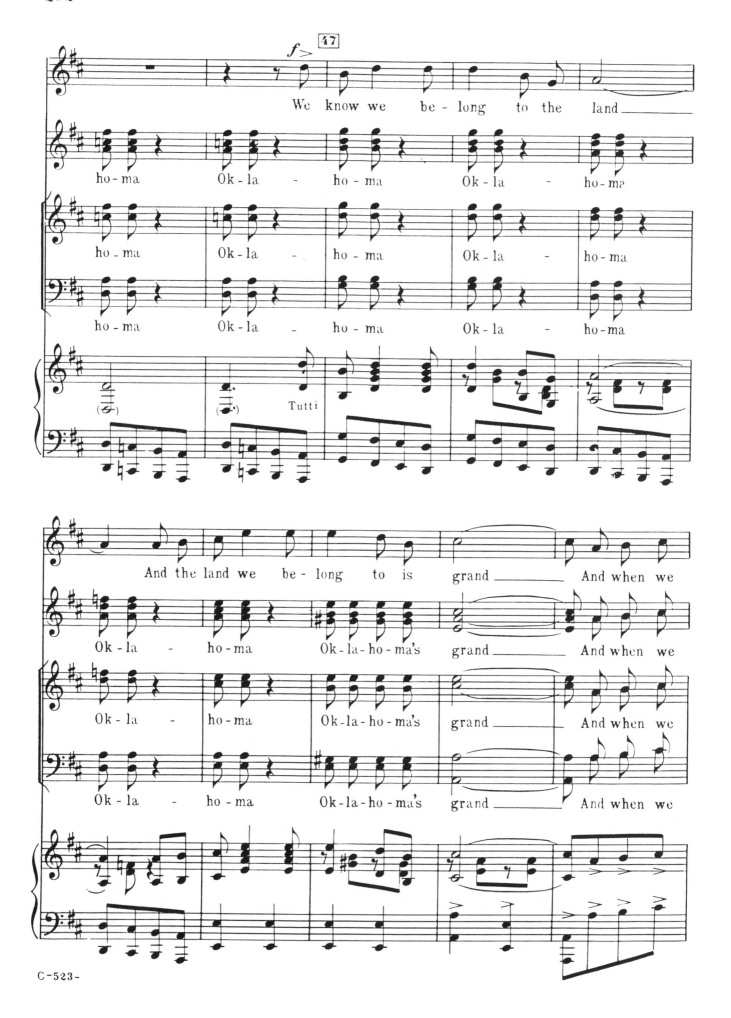

Cue: Annie: "But he explained it fine!"

Oh, what a beau-ti-ful day _____

25 *(Laurey is lifted into the surrey. Curly climbs up alongside her)*

I got a beau-ti-ful feel - in'

(The men start to pull the surrey off, Curly and Laurey waving back at the crowd. The curtain falls before the

Ev - 'ry-thin's go - in' my way _____

surrey is off-stage)

Oh, what a beau-ti-ful day _____

ff

First Curtain

37 Moderato

Tutti

Curtain up

The characters on stage as the first curtain fell, have regrouped.

ENTIRE COMPANY: *(They break the picture and line up to sing. All the other characters enter for this final picture.)*

Peo - ple will say we're in love, ___

Don't start ___ col - lect - ing things ___

Give me my rose and my glove ___

Sweet - heart ___ they're sus - pect - ing things ___

Final Curtain

Peo - ple will say we're in love. ___

Fine Ultimo

Outmarch

No 30

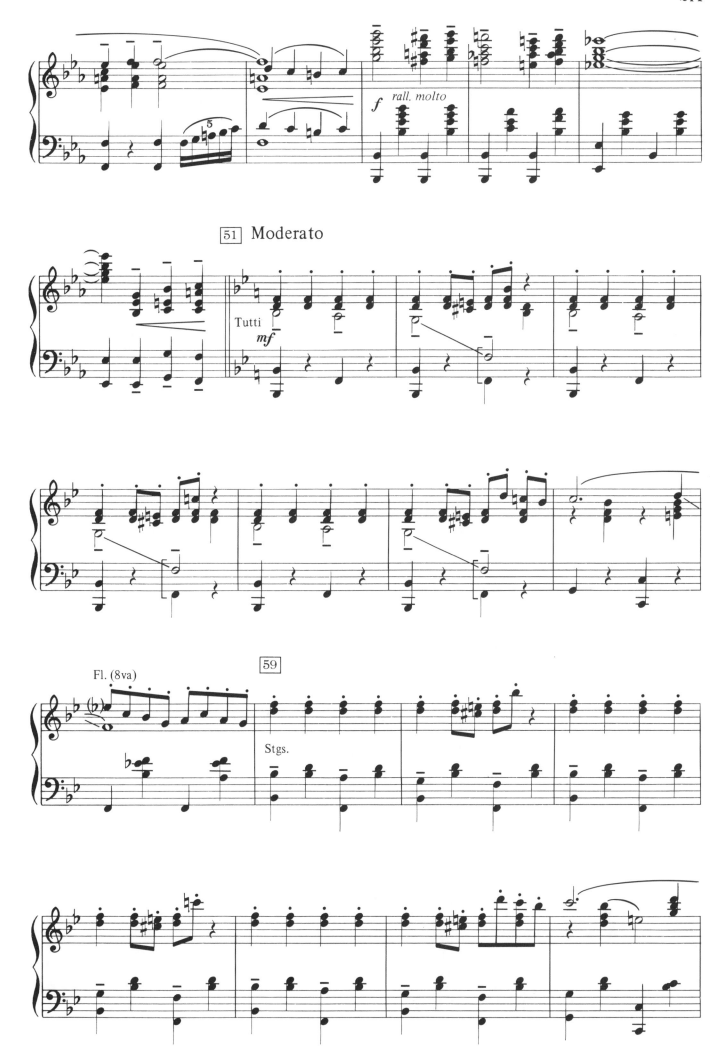